i & i

Chase Those Crazy Baldheads

Out of Town

Library of Congress Control Number:

ISBN-13: 978-1500499761
ISBN: 10: 1500499765

CONTENTS

FORWARD

IT'S JUST LUNCH

Or: *A Small Book with a Big Ideal.*

Trust me, I am fully aware about how you feel. When someone told you about a "crazy baldhead manifesto" book, you probably thought it was a joke. Then they mentioned that it is a book about politics, and your eyes glazed over with boredom. I know, I know—politicians. You don't like 'em; you don't trust 'em; you don't want 'em. But you need 'em! Sounds like the lyrics to a good country-western song.

I was the same way once. Truth be told, I still have my moments. But I came to realize that if someone has the power to detain me, put surveillance on me, tax me, determine the quality of the food I eat and the air I breathe, and regulate my alcohol, tobacco, and firearms, then it's probably a good idea to help keep an eye on them.

I don't claim to have a long prestigious resume on political thought and analysis. *I am everyday people, fighting for solutions to everyday people's problems.* I just thought it was time to put down in writing the way I believe most people feel. It's time to chase those crazy baldheads out of town!

Easy now! All of the Michael Jordan, Vin Diesel, and Bruce Willis

i

fans can calm down. That is not a fashion statement. Baldness, of course, is a metaphor. I equate each positive action with a strand of hair. Act in good faith to maintain your campaign promises—a strand. Willingness to vote for or against an action that would negatively impact your *personal political interest*—a few more strands of hair. Work to find a balanced approach to tough issues—even more strands of hair.

Analyzing the current political class under these guidelines reveals a lot of bald. I'm talking slick Bean City bald. Becoming Independent & Involved (I & I) is the Rogaine solution for this motley crew.

So invest one lunch—just one. After reading this crazy baldhead manifesto, you may want to become Independent & Involved or maybe not. If nothing else it will help you to chew a little slower and will help you to digest your lunch a little easier.

1

THREE BULLETS TO THE HEAD!

Or: The Current State of Dysfunction in Our Political Process

So why should you waste your valuable time and read this book—even worse spend your time on a book about politics? Well, first of all, it's short! Secondly, something of yours has been broken—something very valuable. This is how you file the claim to get it fixed. Finally, yet most importantly, it affects you and everyone you care about. Your health, safety, and financial well-being depend on it.

You see, whether by birth or by choice you are blessed to live in a country where the people and institutions that govern you can be moved. Once they are heard, policy will reflect the voices of the citizens they represent. Here's the problem.

The people who control these institutions and government agencies (let's call them "peeps") have a big hearing problem. If they can't hear your voice, you don't have access. Currently, the only way to turn on the hearing aid and gain access is with dollars—either directly to the candidate or through a lobbyist organization.

Think of it this way: that pretty girl you want to meet is high maintenance! So you either need to be rich or have a good wingman (the lobbyist) to help you close the deal. Don't have either? Then you, my friend, are "short!"

How did our system get so twisted? Why are the institutions and government structures getting worse and less effective at problem solving? Why do we keep electing the same knuckleheads that banter back forth on cable news shows or online blogs? Will it ever change? Unlikely—at least not without an intervention. That's the ugly truth. Want to know why? There are three key reasons it is unlikely to change on its own. Are you ready for these jagged little bullets?

"The Domino Effect": Intervention to the current political process is required. If not the domino effect, the three bullets will continue until the system entirely collapses upon itself.

#1 "Gerrymandering"

That's just a fifty-cent word for rigging the playing field so the "odds are in their (the incumbent politicians') favor." Once in power, they vote to modify districts so that all of the politically like-minded people are lumped into one area or district. That of course would be the district that they want to represent. This problem has been getting progressively worse since the 1980s. Now, with current technology, this can be done so precisely that you can split counties, neighborhoods, and even the middle of a street to maximize the desired result. And guess what: it's perfectly legal.

Below is a map of the Fourth Congressional District of Illinois. Take a glance at the map, and this point becomes painfully obvious. The shaded areas are the boundaries of the district. That big patch of real estate in the middle? That is where they believe the citizens are who don't "think like" or who have not traditionally supported the representative for this district. It would seem obvious that due to their geographic alignment these folks would share some interests in common: schools, roads, bridges— something! Not according to the "peeps": "Let's just cut 'em and gut 'em. It's too much work to try to gain some consensus. They are probably thinking "I need to get back to DC. I have a tee time at Congressional course this weekend." Ah, it's a good life for the political peeps.

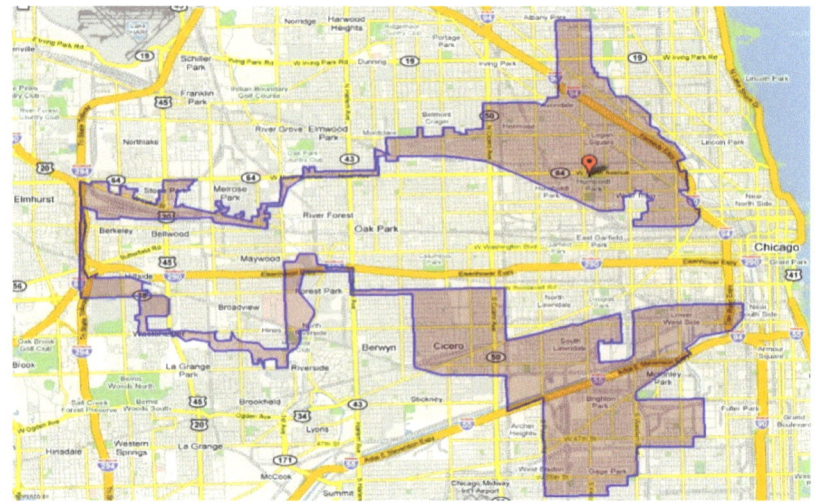

"Our Kind of People": The Fourth Congressional District of Illinois (circa 2010), one of the most Gerrymandered districts in the United States

The next bullet is quite a doozy. We have to look at the man in the mirror for this one. It also reminds me of the first marriage counseling session my wife and I had after seven years of marriage: "You're the problem." "No, *you're* the problem." "No, *you're* the problem"—on and on for sixty minutes. (By the way, we have been married over twenty-seven years!) But I digress.

#2 You're the Problem

Apathy about our elected officials and accountability for their lack of performance have been virtually nonexistent in recent history. Since 1964 the reelection rate has averaged over 90 percent for incumbents in the senate and in the house of representatives (center for responsive politics, 1964-2012 Congressional Reelection Rates opensecrets.org/bigpicture/reelect.php). How's that for job security? That means that no matter how many bonehead mistakes you make or decisions you refuse to make, these folks from that Gerrymandered district keep sending you back. Why? Because it is not my guy that's the problem; it's your (everyone else's) guy that's the problem. In actuality, *you* are the problem. Ouch, I know that hurt. But it is true.

Last, but surely not least: the cream on the top of this kerfuffle. (That a nice way to say that a situation is *fubar*. Don't know that one either? Google it!) This one is my favorite bullet. Why? For one reason, it has many different aliases and phrases that I could have used to describe it: "show me the money," "cashing out," "Big Daddy Warbucks," and I could go on for hours.

The other reason this is my favorite is because it has such an overwhelming influence in our process. It's kind of like Georgia kudzu. Kudzu is a fast-growing green weed that once firmly established will overtake and kill everything in its path! So many names, so few pages. Alas, I settled on the one that best describes the end result of money and politics because most of us end up getting soaked!

3 Making It Rain!

The Supreme Court's decisions of *Buckley v. Valeo* in 1976 and *Citizens United v. Federal Election Commissions* in 2010 cemented money's role in politics: *the leading role*. The *Valeo* decision allows an individual to spend an unlimited amount of money on one or as many candidates as that individual chooses.

The *Citizens United* decision basically says that "corporations are people too," and they can spend in the same way.

"Piglitician": Great benefits, full pension, free airport parking, a 90 percent job security rating! What a job (US Senate/HOR since 1964)!

So there it is. The three principles of politics that are not going to change on their own. These three things are to a politician what OxyContin or heroin are to a drug addict. They've got it bad, and that ain't good.

Together they are clouding up the inner workings of our legislative process and making severe problems chronic and chronic problems terminal. If, as Americans, we are one in the "body politic," gerrymandering, lack of accountability, and money have hit us hard. We are alive but in critical condition—thanks to three bullets to the head.

ALEX, I'LL TAKE CIVICS FOR $200 PLEASE

Or: *The Low-Information Voter*

Here is your first gut check. Let me be perfectly clear. An uninformed voter (UV), or in some cases a low-information voter (LIV), does not necessarily mean dumb. It just means that he or she chooses not to spend a reasonable amount of time thinking about, discussing, or acting upon the things that can impact his or her lives through the actions taken via the political process. Things such as health, safety, privacy, education, taxes, and more. Some simply choose to press the "ignore" button.

They are like little puppies who get distracted by something shiny because the real prize is hidden from their view. *Dancing with the Stars, American Idol, Video Gaming, Real Housewives, or Duck Dynasty*—these are only a few of the many shiny objects available to us. More people can tell you last year's Academy Awards nominees for best picture or the latest NASCAR standings than can name a member of congress or a member of the president's cabinet.

I confess: I am no angel when it comes to looking at shiny things. Yep, I'm old school—football fan. The *NFL Red Zone* is seven hours of commercial-free football. I can go into my man cave and not come out for at least ten hours. (There is a Sunday night game as well. It has commercials, but by that time I am in a full-on all-day bender.) It is so addictive that I am amazed at how fast the day and part of the night goes by. It's like visual cocaine. I've never used it myself, but according to the late R&B artist Rick James, "Cocaine is a hell of drug!"

We all have things that we would rather do than deal with the nature of politics. After all, it means dealing with people who act and think different from ourselves—dealing with the minutiae of laws and regulations, protocol, policies, and procedures. Frankly, at times it can be very, *very* boring. *Unfortunately, the three bullets in our collective head required us to change our focus.*

I force myself to read articles, listen to alternative radio, and *seek out shows that provide me a reasonable understanding about what the people who are taxing, spying, regulating, and spending are up to.*

We can no longer just vote for a party (or candidate) every few years and hope that they will do the right thing. Because in the end, they *will* do the right thing. It's just *the right thing for them* personally. Believe that! This is "Final Jeopardy" for all of us, especially for the low-information voter.

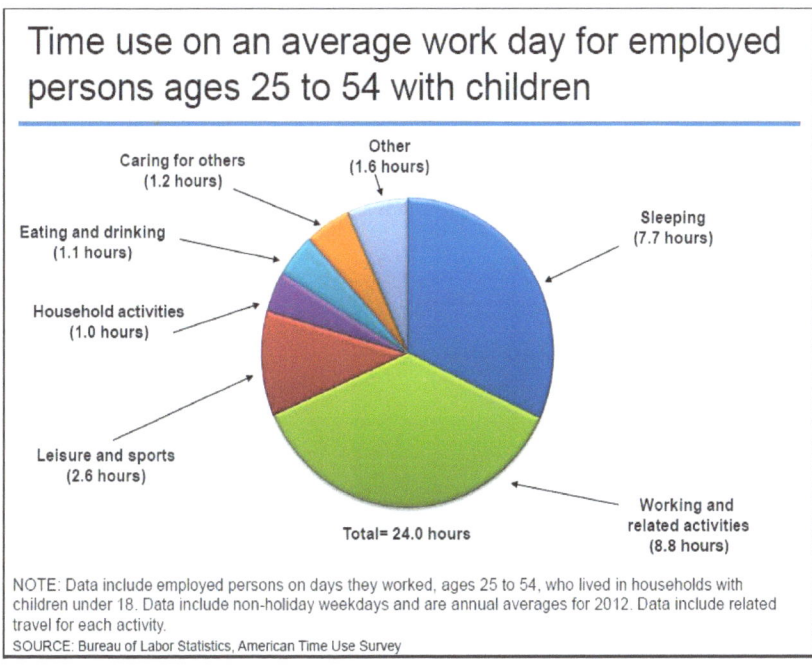

Time use on an average work day for employed persons ages 25 to 54 with children

Caring for others (1.2 hours)
Other (1.6 hours)
Sleeping (7.7 hours)
Eating and drinking (1.1 hours)
Household activities (1.0 hours)
Leisure and sports (2.6 hours)
Total= 24.0 hours
Working and related activities (8.8 hours)

NOTE: Data include employed persons on days they worked, ages 25 to 54, who lived in households with children under 18. Data include non-holiday weekdays and are annual averages for 2012. Data include related travel for each activity.
SOURCE: Bureau of Labor Statistics, American Time Use Survey

"No Time for Foolishness": Stressful American lives leave little time for political analysis

President John F. Kennedy once said: "The ignorance of one voter in a democracy impairs the security of all." Yikes, blow the whistle! We are at condition *fubar*! Most Americans can name the three stooges, but not the three branches of government (Zogby Poll 2006). That same poll stated that most Americans can name two of the seven dwarfs but not two Supreme Court justices. Yep, these are registered voters.

Wait—it gets worse. An even smaller percentage of registered voters actually vote. According to the *Washington Post*, 42 percent of registered voters cast a ballot in 2010. In 2012 almost ninety million Americas who were eligible to vote did not. The checks and balances for our politicians have all checked out! When you combine low participation with low information, it equals low accountability and high job security for politicians.

Dr. Ben Carson, a renowned surgeon who practiced in the Baltimore area, has been urged to seek political office. While he has declined to run for any office to date, he offered this interesting comment about LIVs and the political process: "Quite frankly, having an uninformed populace works extremely well (for politicians), particularly when you have a media that doesn't understand its responsibility and feels more like it's an arm of a political party. They can really take advantage of uninformed populace."

Let not your heart be troubled! The people who support being I & I don't care about your past knowledge. We care about your future actions. Your future is getting brighter and stronger!

"Trust Me": Low Voter participation + Low Information + Low Accountability = Job security for politicians

According to the 2010 census, there are about 150 million registered voters in the United States. There are over 207 million that are eligible—a difference of 57 million. These individuals are who you call the "hard-core shiny ball folks." It is clear: some people choose to ignore, can't grasp, or don't care about the political process. Others can't discern the political process. If you care and have a desire to become involved I believe that you are special.

I believe that you have a gift—the gifts of inquisitiveness and discernment because you have been given these gifts. Guess what? To whom much is given, much is required. That means that you have to do the heavy lifting and act in the best interests of everyone—not just your own interests. Otherwise, you are acting just like the "peeps" that created the current dysfunctional process we have now.

Our goal should be to try to add as many people to the political process as possible. But I don't believe in dragging folks to the water. If they become thirsty, they can walk to the well like everyone else. Once Independents use their leverage to create change, people will jump onboard. When the train leaves the station, they can choose whether or not to jump on the I & I train. They are welcome. But we need not make any unscheduled stops to pick them up. Time is limited. We are in the ICU, and its code red. Even a low-information voter can understand that.

3

BUST A MOVE!

Or: *Low Voter Sentiment Provides Opportunity for Change*

By now you probably feel like you are drinking water from a fire hydrant. If you've never really put any serious thought about these issues before it can be a little intimidating.

Let's recap. The entire process has seized up. People are uninformed. Politicians are self-centered, and money is controlling everyone in the process. Yep, I think that about wraps it up.

Hold on, don't panic! There's no need to prepare for a worldwide apocalypse. The tables are about to turn. Our table is being set up for success. We are not alone in our frustration. A record-high 42 percent of Americans identify themselves as Independents (Gallup 2014). It is reasonable to assume that this same percentage translates to registered voters. If we can convert and engage an additional total of 10 percent each from the other "major" parties, we will have established a *quorum* of the voting public. We just need to start climbing the mountain of despair that has become our political process. If we were to compare this process to climbing a mountain, we would be at base camp, ready to make our final push for the summit of the mountain. Once we are at the summit—"it's a wrap"—we can take back our political process.

Enlightening several million people, in the past, that would have been a very tall task. Not in today's world. Consider the retweets of the Ellen DeGeneres "selfie" viewed over thirty-seven million times. It caused the Twitter site to crash. We are wired and connected to each other. We have portable computers with us all the time. Some would say too much of the time. There are a lot of shiny balls to play with on cell phones. It doesn't matter. We have the right message. This is the right time. So let's bust a move toward reclaiming our political process.

"Connected": Social Media creates the perfect platform to launch and motivate others to create political and social change.

NOT THAT THERE'S ANYTHING WRONG WITH THAT!

Or: *The Political Elite Count on Voter Apathy to Maintain Power*

Still reading? You passed the first hurdle. Now it's time for gut check #2. There's no stopping us now! Let's keep climbing a little further toward the summit. For those of you who are not fans of *Seinfeld*, the title phrase for this section may be a little strange. It comes from an episode titled "The Outing." A reporter thinks Jerry (Jerry Seinfeld) and his best friend George (Jason Alexander) are a *gay* couple after a joke that takes place at their favorite coffee shop. The episode hinges around Jerry's response to people thinking that he is gay.

He wants to correct them while not appearing to be homophobic—because he isn't. In short, it's an easy way to say: *That's not* me, *but it's cool if that's* you. When you mention politics you normally find that most people either get angry or get bored. If you have read this far, I know that you are not bored—perplexed, maybe, but not bored. But wait, there is still time!

The water is going to get a little deeper now. It's getting clearer. You can see that to move forward you will have to move from thought to action and from words to deeds. In less poetic terms, get up off your ass and do something—or not. This is the last paragraph of this manifesto that some people will ever read. This is the part when the pages start to close. Folks say to themselves, *I don't like the way things are, but I would like someone else to do it for me.* They acknowledge that change will require more than poetic speeches and catch phrases. "Change you can believe in" can only come from *you*: if *you* ask, *you* watch,, and *you* challenge. It will mean sending a few more e-mails, logging a few more posts, and staying on top of issues between election cycles—i.e., effort. It will require wisdom to seek balance in our public policies. It will require strength to act in the interests of the good folks who don't share your gifts but who will be impacted by your actions. Don't be confused. *Freedom is free, but there is a cost. You have to pay attention.* For some that price is too high. Not that there is anything wrong with that.

4

THE CHOICE

THE RED PILL VERSUS THE BLUE PILL?

Or: *Choosing to Activate Your Gifts*

Right now you are probably feeling like Alex in Wonderland, or in this case, it's more like "Reality-land." Just like in the movie *The Matrix* (1999 Warner Brothers), the case has been put before you. Morpheus (Laurence Fishburne) has exposed the truth: a poorly performing education system, massive debt, big brother surveillance, immigration woes, the military industrial complex— it's a very long list. The framework our founding fathers created to control these problems is itself out of control. There is nothing but trouble in our way. There is no time to assess blame—no one on your right or your left to put the pieces back together again. If it is to be, it must be me.

Take the blue pill—end of story. You can go back to letting others legislate the decisions that affect the lives of you and your loves ones. It's okay that you may not have the gifts. You'll be fine. There are a lot of different types of shiny balls for you to play with. For some folks, that is more than enough, and it's a very good life.

Take the red pill, and you stay in "Reality-land." You have seen that the body politic has taken three bullets to the head, gerrymandering, apathy toward accountability, and big money. It will not be easy. There will be some struggles and a lot of pushback from those in power. After all, to the political elite everything is coming up roses. For you and me it is just the thorns. It is decision time my friend. It's time to choose: red or blue?

"Choose": "Remember, all I'm offering is the truth. Nothing else." —Morpheus

5

NOW THAT'S REAL TALK

Or: *Solutions Using Centrist Policies and Pragmatism*

One thing that bothers me about today's political discourse is the righteousness of it. Everyone thinks that they have the "right" answer, when in fact, they don't. It's just "an" answer, which at any given time could be placed on a continuum from absolute right to absolute wrong. We are bound by our human nature. We only see a problem from the perspectives that we have experienced in our lives or from those individuals we directly interact with.

We may work with unemployed folks having a hard time getting a job. But we don't see the ones who are gaming the system and passing on a job—a job that may not be an "ideal" way. But it is "a" way. In the 2012–13 reporting period, the state of North Carolina reported over $225 million in improper payments for unemployment insurance (US Dept. of Labor). Yep, one state, one year.

We may disagree with environmentalists trying to stop a mining company from bringing jobs to a community. But we fail to see the hypocrisy in allowing that same company to write key segments of the laws allowing that mining project, even to the point that the mining company can veto or exempt itself from any requirements, without public oversight and input (Wisconsin. Bad River Watershed AB 426/SB 488).

We may believe that Medicare and Medicaid should be expanded to meet the needs of the poor. But does it make sense to blindly throw money into a system that routinely pays over $22 billion in improper payments. Yep, I said *billion* (US Office of Management and Budget 2008). They paid dead physicians on over 478,000 claims, totaling over $92 million (US Senate Permanent Committee on Investigations 2008).

The list of waste fraud and abuse goes on and on. Everyone wants to limit the problem. But everyone flinches when it is time to cut their piece of the pie. I believe that this is not due to selfishness, but a lack of trust that the pain will be shared proportionally.

Politicians inability to manage properly further exacerbates the ineffective use of the public's tax dollars. They never set up performance metrics or continuous improvement mechanisms. Instead of rewarding whistleblowers, they are routinely harassed, outcast or even jailed.

Logic tells us that a problem first must be controlled to be solved.

The majority of citizens will allow and tolerate a balanced approach. They will push back if they feel policies are too extreme in one direction or another. The problem is that we can no longer vote left one cycle and right the next to try to achieve that balance—been there, done that. We need a new vision and a new direction.

A revolution of independence and involvement by a quorum of registered voters will force legislators into balanced governance. If not, they will face recall or rejection during the next voting cycle. Why? Because now we have a quorum that pays attention and remembers to hold you accountable. And we will. Now that's real talk!

6

I'M GOING TO STOP PLAYING WITH YOUR SHINY BALLS NOW!

Or: *The Case for Political Independence as a Strategy for Change*

Outstanding! I'm glad to see you are still hanging in there. You are close to helping us achieve the quorum we need to fix our damaged processes. Hopefully you are starting to feel a little irked—getting mad about being played for a fool. You are not alone. A 2013 public policy poll rated the congressional approval rating slightly below cockroaches and traffic jams. Hmm…I think folks might be a little upset.

Are you wondering why I have not mentioned Democrat or Republican, conservative or liberal, left or right? Because it does not matter. First of all, this left–right thing is a false paradigm. The "peeps" all went to the same schools, dine at the same restaurants, attend the same social functions, are members of the same clubs, or share the same donors to their campaign. Boy, do they share the same donors.

The chart below ("Double Down") is just a snapshot of what occurs across the nation. Big money donors claim that they are helping to contribute to a healthy political process. I call it buttering both sides of the bread! Get it? Money, bread, butter? Yea, that one is a little weak! *But I digress!*

Riddle me this: Let's say that you have a question for your congressperson, and a board member from one of the companies on the chart listed on the next page has a question for the same congressperson at the same time. Whose call (e-mail, tweet, fax) is he or she going to respond to? Of course, not yours! Once again, my friend, you are short!

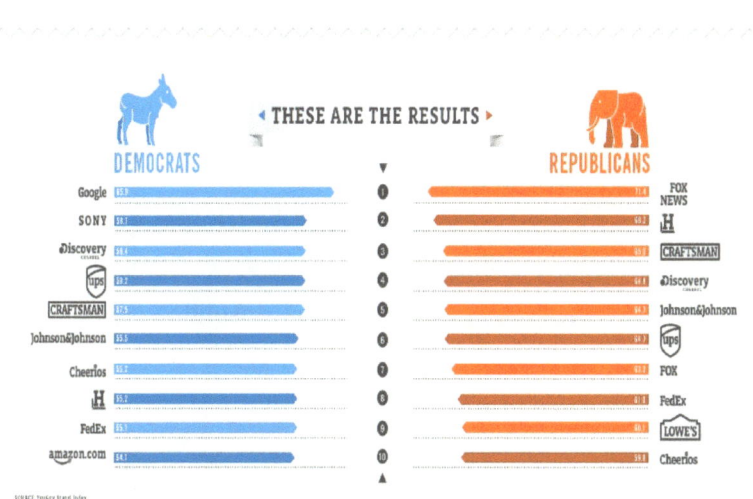

"Double Down": Corporations often hedge influence by contributing to both of the major political parties

For the record I acknowledge that corporations and wealthy individuals have a key role to play in our society. I applaud anyone who has a desire to create wealth. The opportunity to create wealth and to provide for ourselves and our loved ones is a key element of what makes us special. Believe me, I live it. I have a real estate company and a media creative business. Every day is like a scene out of the movie *Jerry McGuire*: "Show me the money!" I have an E-trade account and a few 401(k)s. So I understand that corporations need to make money to pay dividends, which funds my retirement, which keeps me off assistance programs, and which helps to keep the deficit in check. I get that.

Unfortunately, corporations and wealthy individuals too often wield power for their good at the expense of everyone else. They manipulate to keep others from gaining and improving financially due to their talents and ideals. That is not the desire to acquire wealth. That is gluttony of wealth. That is desire for absolute power. The best way to get absolute power is to influence the people who tax you, regulate you, and can arrest or detain you. As we know, absolute power corrupts—absolutely.

I believe that the reason you see so many career politicians is because the "peeps" enjoy the power and the privileges a little too much. So they do just enough to maintain power. They pass on tough decisions because it could hurt their chances for reelection instead of doing what may be in the best interest for the country as a whole.

When is it time for a fresh start, some new ideals, some new blood? In June 2014, Representative Charles Rangel, congressman from Harlem, New York, and Mississippi senator Thad Cochran both won their respective party's nomination for reelection in the fall of the same year. If reelected, this will be Mr. Rangel's twelfth term (twenty-four years) and Mr. Cochran's sixth term (thirty-six years).

Hey, I am on the tail end of the baby boomers, but I relate more to Generation X. I know that if you are healthy, you can be productive later in life. But c'mon, man! When it comes to elected officials, there is no left or right, just power or no power. They chose power. So regardless of your personal politics, why would you pledge blind allegiance to any party or politician? Judge them not on words but deeds.

"'Two Ps (Politicians) in a Pod": Congressman Charlie Rangel (left) and Senator Thad Cochran (right) rank high on the list of legislators with the longest tenure in the US Congress - July 2014

7

USE WHAT YOU'VE GOT TO GET WHAT YOU WANT!

Or: Use the Vote as a Commodity to Counter the Commodity of Money and Influence

The economic engine that drives the United States is capitalism. It is inevitable that money will creep into the political process. The Supreme Court cases I previously mentioned validate the role of capital in politics. Dollars are now a commodity in the political process. They are the dominate commodity. So how do you knock out a giant? With one strategically placed stone.

Riddle me this: How does one man with one hundred dollars and one vote compete with one man with one millions dollars and one vote?

He doesn't—unless he combines with another man and another man and another man to act in unison and shift the rules of the game back to a more neutral position. By acting in unison the votes themselves become a commodity, just like the dollars given by big donors are a commodity. This joint action can negate the impact of unlimited spending in our political process. After all, an individual big-money donor can only vote once!

Let me clarify something. I am not advocating for people to abandon core beliefs and principles. Our primary objective is to withhold support and force a meaningful dialogue on hard choices and reward the politicians who have the courage to support actions that offer a centrist approach. A balanced approach is the only way to implement policies that are sustainable in this current hyperpartisan environment. This is our hold card. What the great soul singer James Brown said then, is just as true now: "Use what you've got to get what you want!"

"Counterweight": Mass exodus from affiliation with both of the major political parties will counter the influence of big money and partisanship

WHEN I MOVE, YOU MOVE!
Or: *The Ripple Effect*

You are probably saying to yourself: *How can we have independent thought and move together?* An excellent question. We do need to move as a block but not necessarily vote as a block. The first *I* in "I & I" is *independence: a massive move away from identification with both of the major political parties toward a registered Independent status with a goal to force our representatives toward a more "open and centrist" campaigning and governing philosophy.*

Think of it this way: in sports, when an athlete is no longer contractually bound to play for a specific team, he or she is considered to be a free agent. The higher the skill set of the free agent, the more other teams will do to entice the athlete to sign with them. They will hire or fire coaches, add new players, release others—all in an effort to gain their services. In addition, when the athlete is productive, these same teams will continue to do things to encourage the free agent to sign again at the end of the contract. If you apply this to being I & I, you, the voter, are the free agent (independence). The teams are the various political parties. The production is your "involvement." Once you "declare" your free agency, the power and control shift to you.

The fact is that most of the voting public is centrist in nature. However, due to the primary (nomination) process, most of these primaries are only open to the "registered members" of the Democrat or Republican parties. That means that the hard-core activists select who the final candidates will be in the general election, limiting the options. That would be like your parents agreeing to handle all of your expenses for your prom, but they get to pick your date!

The goal of being I & I is to force everyone to the middle. We can have a third way without having a third party. Forming another party just means more bureaucracy. When we move independently but as one it will create a shift so tectonic in scale that it will send lasting shock waves through the political system. But this can only happen if when I move, you move.

Don't let your parents pick your prom date. Declare your free agency!

TOO MANY CATS TO CORAL

Or: Encouraging Independent Thought and *Interdependent* Action

On the average, 58–60 percent of eligible voters cast a ballot. In recent history, under the two-party system, about 20 percent of those voters are "in play" or can be swayed to vote for either party. *The actual number is probably much higher*. Why is this? I am sure that we all know someone who is voting Republican or Democrat because that is the way most of the people in their circle of influence are voting. They have a general feeling about a candidate or party, so they are inclined to validate their own position and beliefs. With the proper incentive, information, and motivation, these voters are in play as well. We just need them to *not* focus on the shiny balls of life so much!

Our goal is to increase party defections from the Democrats and Republicans. By reducing the overall number of partisans to an even smaller percentage of the electorate, neither party can produce enough scale to win a general election without compromise. Keeping with our prom example: they can nominate the court, but they can't choose the queen. That means that even with gerrymandered districts they cannot win or get reelected to office without winning an even greater percentage of the Independent vote than in the past. They won't get that vote without a major shift in how they campaign and govern.

This shift requires everyone of every political persuasion to move to a registered Independent status. How do we get them to move? By changing traditional thinking and providing them with a vehicle to do something about it. Think that is crazy—asking a little too much maybe? Crazy is reelecting the same people over and over who "say" one thing while campaigning but "do" another, or nothing at all, when in office.

There is a scene in the movie *I'm Gonna Get You, Sucka* (Front Films 1988) in which the main character, Jack Spade (Keenen Ivory Wayans), convinces a beautiful young lady (Anne-Marie Johnson) to spend the evening with him. Once things get heated, she decides to show the "real" person that she is. She starts removing her padded bra, wig, colored contacts and lots of other things! Yep, your elected officials are acting just like that. So, "let's go crazy."

Another benefit of accountability through involvement is that it helps to neutralize political ads. We know that they use political advertising to hide or distort their true persona. These ads are mostly targeted to move a small percentage of the Independent voters, who are traditionally known as swing voters, and a substantial percentage of them are LIVs. This is when they create a public persona that "appears" to move to the center. They look like a beautiful young lady—only to get elected and start "removing" the positions they showed us before.

Becoming I & I negates that strategy that worked so well in the past. The candidates will realize that they need to start from a more neutral and less partisan position. If not, the volume of swing voters needed to win is simply too great. They can no longer dismiss their rhetoric from the primaries because being I & I means that a substantial portion of the electorate will remind them of what they stated during the primaries. We will point out the hypocrisy of their waffling positions. This will open the channels for a true debate—a debate about what needs to occur to contain the many and pressing issues we face as a country, even if it means painful decisions. It forces them to open themselves up to solutions that would be toxic to the "party base" they leveraged to win a nomination but better for the entire country as a whole. It will be a tough fight. The partisans will fight back because they believe that their answer is the only one.

As for me, I will not allow the chains of traditional thinking to bind me. I would be willing to support policies and laws that have been vetted and debated by the many versus the influence of a few corporations or individuals, even if I personally feel that these policies have some flaws.

At least I know that "we the people" are working toward a more perfect union, not a system where "we the rich," "we the well connected," or "we the corporations" are working against that union and in the interests of themselves.

We know—in our guts we know. We know that to a politician the only thing better that a million-dollar campaign contribution is a million votes. We know that despite the rhetoric, the politicians won't fix it themselves. They can't. The system reeks of backbiting, infighting, and influence peddling. They are addicted to power. Only an intervention in which we shock the system will do. Changing a president or a congressperson one at a time will not work either. That creates divided government; partisanship gouges the wound even deeper. You can't heal bullet wounds until you remove the bullets.

We know—in our guts we know. It is intervention time: time for everyone who cares about the future of our great nation to rise— rise up and use the gifts they have to stop the madness. There is just one question left. In many ways it will be the hardest to resolve as a nation. Polls show that we are ready. We are frustrated, we are angry, and in some cases we are fearful. But, are we willing?

Our finger is on the button, but are we willing to push?

Push the politicians, push ourselves, push each other. Push for solutions that are not perfect but practical. Push until we make the hard decisions that will fundamentally and permanently change the political landscape and strengthen our foundation as a nation and inspire the world. If you are ready to push, push back and push hard. Ready to push using independent thought to create *interdependent* actions? Then you are ready to be Independent & Involved. Then you are ready to use what you've got to get what you want. Solutions.

If the answer is *yes,* congratulations! Your blue pill is fully digested.

Push! *"Free your mind, and the rest will follow."* —En Vogue

8

I KNOW WHAT YOU DID LAST SUMMER

Or: *Involvement Begets Awareness; Awareness Begets Accountability*

Freedom Works is a mostly conservative political action committee. They have a motto that rings true: "Government goes to those who show up." When the only people who show up are those with a financial incentive or a moral agenda that fits their world paradigm, creative solutions get sacrificed on the altar of selfishness. For our political system to work, balance must be imposed from the outside by its citizenry. Involvement is the yin, the bricks, the lock. Independence is the yang, the mortar, the key.

Okay, let's keep it real! It sounds good on paper so far, right? The problem, quite frankly, is that working toward this balance can at times be very, very boring.

Riddle me this: If you were at the water cooler at work and someone asked you, "What do you think about the proposed changes to Article 343 of Section 403 of Chapter IV of the FDA's Food, Drug, and Cosmetic Act?" you would think they are smoking crack cocaine (yea, we know that cocaine is a hell of a drug*). But I digress!* All of that legal mumbo jumbo is pretty boring, right? What if I asked the same question this way: "The house is considering rule changes that would change meat labeling requirements—you know, the guidelines that keep you from buying dog meat labeled as hamburger? Now that I've got your attention…."

"Yin & Yang": "Based on Chinese philosophy of interconnectivity. Yin and yang can be thought of as complementary (rather than opposing) forces that interact to form a dynamic system in which the whole is greater than the assembled parts." —Wikipedia

Nonetheless, I am a realist. This attention will be temporary for most of us. Fortunately there are people and organizations who do this heavy lifting for us. I call them "the watchers," and I have provided a great list of resources at the back of the manifest to help you to get started on your journey. In order to maximize the good work that these individuals and organizations do, we must create delivery systems of information that will activate enough registered voters to get a quorum.

We need a comprehensive strategy that will focus on a few guiding elements that can create momentum with minimal effort by those who are I & I. The key, and this is an important one, is that we have to do it without boring them to death. I'm thinking something like *The Daily Show* meets "WikiLeaks" with a side of Tumblr. All guided by five key principles:

1. Clear ballot access guidelines

2. Updated registration status

3. Leverage technology effectively

4. Reward compromise

5. Encourage creative solutions

THE FIVE GUIDING PRINCIPLES OF BEING I & I

1. PUT ME IN THE GAME, COACH!
Or: *Open Ballots Can Open Minds*

Having fair access to as many ballots as possible will help to level the playing field currently dominated by the two mainstream parties. Both parties want to limit the choices. Republicans and Democrats routinely sue to keep additional choices off the ballot. Choice will increase the opportunity for creative solutions via more candidates to enter into the discussion. We should support laws that promote viable Independent candidacy and advocate laws that are clear and can be validated. I personally feel that anyone who meets the established criteria for a given state should be put on the ballot.

However, the goal of being I & I is not necessarily to vote for an alternative-party candidate. *It is to vote for the "best" candidate who will vote to govern with courage on the hard choices that need to be made.* That may be an individual of one of the established parties, or it may not be. If past performance indicates future behavior, the choice will eventually become clear. It will be a come-to-Jesus moment for the establishment. After all, self-preservation is the one thing politicians understand most. You may see a deathbed conversion once the tide turns. When politicians feel the winds of change, they will alter their sails accordingly.

2. REP YOUR CITY!
Or: *Change Your Registration Status to Independent*

We have been discussing this throughout the book, so there's no great reveal for this guiding principle. The ability to demonstrate to the electoral elite that independent thought is the new normal is a bold statement. We will make it loudly. Declaring to "opt out" on your voting profile is important. In most states this can be done easily by contacting your state board of elections. If this can't be done easily, well, you have your first assignment.

3. THERE IS AN APP FOR THAT!
Or: *Leverage Technology and Media Creatively to Promote Involvement*

This will be the biggest challenge we have by far. How do we inform the voters with centrist tendencies on a topic that can be boring for most of them? How can we create a tool that helps the voters reconcile what politicians say versus what they do? How do we track what they did last summer, the previous summer, and every summer through each term? We have started to develop some electronic tools that can assist with this directive. This directive requires IT expertise, so we need help! I could not write code if my life depended on it. Reading this book, you may think that I can't write—period! *But I digress!*

Most people can learn faster and with better recall if the delivery method is a visual one. I asked my IT friends to give me an overview of the process in visual terms. Not! Big miss! The decision points and flow charts are a bit too much to discuss in a manifesto. But I can encapsulate the intent of the tool. In short, the program is a combination fact checker and promise keeper balance sheet. If you claim a position while campaigning but switch that position while in office, it impacts the rating in a negative way. It works the same way for any commitments made. Remember, being I & I means that we support centrist policies, but we support the voice of the people as well. Therefore, a legislator would not be punished for voting in a manner that supports his or her commitments, even though they are not centrist. But the final overall rating would be lower.

For example, let's assume that we have a piece of immigration legislation that is in its final form, has been independently evaluated, and is considered too progressive (liberal). That means there are not enough controls or it is not practical enough to be considered centrist. We have a congressperson who ran a get-tough-on-immigration campaign. If that congressperson voted no, he or she would score a neutral to slightly negative rating: neutral because the people who elected him or her have a right to be represented; slightly negative because he or she did not work with his or her counterparts to secure a balanced centrist bill.

The same scoring relationship works the same for legislation that is at the opposite end of that spectrum. We now have a second piece of immigration legislation.

This bill in its final form is independently evaluated and is considered to be too restrictive (conservative) or too harsh to be centrist. Remember, this legislator ran on an anti-immigration agenda. If the legislator voted yes, he or she would score a neutral to slightly negative rating because he or she voted the way he or she campaigned, but the bill is not centrist.

When up for reelection, a politician's entire record or a specific bill could be easily evaluated. Individuals who are I & I would vote to chase the baldhead out of town whose voting scores are at either end of the spectrum. This system has the two key elements needed for acceptance by the quorum. It is easy to understand, and we have trust. The quorum will trust the scores because they know where we stand on every issue—in the middle.

This puts a value on the behaviors that we have talked about previously in this manifesto: reward courage and centrist-minded legislation. Penalize partisanship and self-centered legislation. This method of gauging the performance of a legislator is called the "Bipartisan Solutions Meter"—yep, a BS meter. Sorry, ladies, this program will not be applicable for use with your male friends.

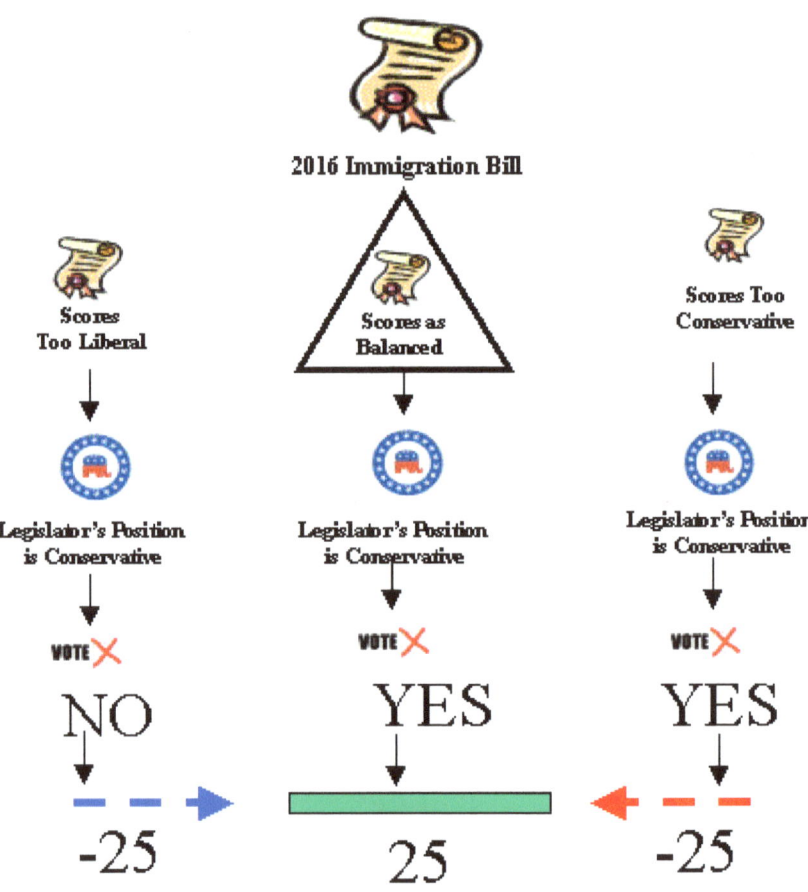

Bipartisan Solutions Meter (BS Meter): The tool compares a legislator's rhetoric versus his or her voting record. The more centrist the voting record, the higher the score.

4. CAN'T WE ALL JUST GET ALONG!

Or: *Reestablish the Dignity of Compromise in the Realm of Governing*

According to Robert Draper in the book *Do Not Ask What Good We Do*, on the night of Barack Obama's inauguration, just over fifteen high-ranking leaders of the Republican party met to plot a campaign to cripple the effectiveness of the administration: a no-honeymoon strategy of all-out resistance to a popular president-elect during an economic emergency. "If he was for it," former Ohio senator George Voinovich explained, "we had to be against it." Ain't partisanship grand?

That's like having an affair with one of the bridesmaids at the wedding reception. The marriage is doomed, and the divorce will be pretty nasty! Trust me, I have my issues with several of President Obama's policies. But this further illustrates why a massive intervention is needed. The inmates are running the asylum.

Ironically, in the past this kind of opposition would be normal behavior, but not now. This was not a normal time by any stretch of the imagination. The nation was in dire straits. This was the beginning of the worst worldwide shock to financial markets since the great depression.

The fall of 2008 was a period in which the major financial markets lost more than 30 percent of their value—a period that ranks among the most horrific in US financial market history.

Part of the same crew that put three bullets in our collective heads—yea, those guys—they are playing games…again! People are losing homes and jobs at an alarming rate. Widespread panic is starting to gain momentum. Under these conditions, what was their primary concern—the first order of business? Power and how to get it back as fast as possible. That's disgusting—just pathetic.

The eyes of the world were on us, awaiting our lead. That should have been a time for men and women of goodwill to seek to truly honor the oath of their office: a time for new thinking; a time for a new resolve to get back on the right track; a time to go *big*; a time to put country first. Instead, they threw gasoline on a raging fire. They chose small: my party, my community, my job, my donors.

When you speak to those around you about becoming I & I, just point out these last few pages. It should be enough to take their eyes off the shiny balls that are distracting them from truth.

"House of Cards": The fall of 2008: a period in which the major financial markets lost more than 30 percent of their value, Republicans plotted to regain power of the house and senate

Six years later, we are still knee deep in this toxic environment of partisanship. Compromise is viewed as either the purview of the weak or the unwise. This is foolish when you consider the interconnectivity of financial markets and the diversity of the people in those markets. Our *current* political thought can be summed up under these two quotations:

"Compromise makes a good umbrella, but a poor roof; it is temporary expedient, often wise in party politics, almost sure to be unwise; in statesmanship." —James Russell Lowell (1819–1891), American poet, critic, editor

"It is the weak man who urges compromise—never the strong man." — Elbert Hubbard (1859–1915), American author, publisher

Yep, in 2008 our elected officials were still thinking and acting like it was the 1800s. Maybe someone should tell them that the world is a much different place. Today the movement of people and the exchanging of ideals are expanding at a rapid pace. We must force balance into our current systems and organizational structures. They are not sustainable as they are currently operating. Obviously, on a personal level, comprise is not desired. Don't settle for the things that could have negative repercussions for you individually, especially when they are under your control. But in terms of public governance, you have to give something to get something. Our *desired* political thought can be summed up under these two quotations:

"Life cannot subsist in modern society but by reciprocal concessions." — **Samuel Johnson**

"Better a diamond with a flaw than a pebble without." —Confucius

5. ALL OF US ARE SMARTER THAN ANY ONE OF US!

Or: *The Smartest Guy in the Room Is Part of an Even Smarter Team*

Don't fool yourself. We will not have a mandate on many of the hard issues. If it were easy, the political elite would have done it by now—or maybe not. In May 2014 the New York state senate went into a debate on making yogurt the official state snack. Now I am sure that the potato chip lobby and the peanut gallery had great consternation about this bill. But come on, man! State assemblies are only in session for a few months a year. They chose to spend part of that time debating yogurt. Seriously? Really? *But I digress*!

To get a consensus on legislation we need to focus on the aggregation of thoughts/ideas/policies and experiences of the centrist-leaning electorate. We won't get every policy right the first time, but a centrist governing philosophy will create policies that allow for course correction and unforeseen consequences. Most importantly, any policy that tackles big issues must be tolerated by the masses. People will deal with a lot of hardship as long as they feel that the pain is being shared proportionally. Centrist governing by its very nature is proportional.

9

LUNCHTIME IS OVER!

Or: Are You Ready to Go to Work?

If anyone other than my wife is reading this paragraph, and you are ready to go to work…hope is still alive. My hope is that you see the hard choices and adult decisions you as a registered voter will have to force your elected officials to make.

Despite the many ignoble aspects of America's history, despite the mistakes and righteous indignation of some of our policies around the world, don't be confused. We are still the world's brightest hope. We don't guarantee success, but we guarantee the opportunity to achieve it. This is the one country that can show how a free and diverse populous can live together and prosper—despite that diversity. It's the reason people risk life and limb, beg and borrow, and cheat and steal to come to our shores.

Every great generation has to make a sacrifice. Through World Wars I and II, the greatest generation gave blood and treasure. Now the baby boomers, the most creative, most enlightened, and most prosperous generation to date must give time and treasure.

Will you be one of the quorum that we need for this change? Are you willing to carve out a few hours each week to look away from the shiny balls of life—enough time to make sure that you have the access and the tools required to leverage the voices of like-minded people? Change will create some voices of doubt: naysayers that will try to weaken your resolve. They know that doubt kills more dreams more often than failure could ever attempt to. Cast them aside. Listen to the voices of like-minded people—people who demand that a government designed by the people is for the people and has the people's interest in mind. So, I'm ready to go to work. Are you? Are you ready to help me chase those crazy baldheads out of town? If the answer is yes! Share this manifest with someone your care about, and get to work!

"In any moment of decision, the best thing you can do is the right thing. The worst thing you can do is nothing." —Theodore Roosevelt

The Man Who Thinks He Can —Walter D. Wintle

If you think you are beaten, you are;

If you think you dare not, you don't.
If you'd like to win, but think you can't,
It's almost a cinch you won't.

If you think you'll lose, you've lost.

For out in the world we find
Success begins with a fellow's will:
It's all in his state of mind.

If you think you're outclassed, you are:

You've got to think high to rise,
You've got to be sure of yourself before
You'll ever win that prize.

Life's battles don't always go

To the stronger or faster man,
But sooner or later the man who wins
Is the one who thinks he can.

RESOURCES FOR "CENTRIST" CHANGE

NETWORK WITH LIKE-MINDED CENTRISTS

WWW. INDEPENDENTVOTING.ORG

WWW.INDEPENDENTVOTERSOFAMERICA.ORG

WWW.INDEPENDENTVOICE.ORG

―――――――

EXPOSING WASTE, HYPERPARTISAN POLITICS

CITIZENS AGAINST GOVERNMENT WASTE
WWW.CAGW.ORG

WWW.OPENSECRETS.ORG

WWW.BLACKBOXVOTING.ORG

―――――――

CENTRIST POLICY ORGANIZATIONS

WWW.THIRDWAY.ORG

WWW.NOLABELS.ORG

www.ingramcontent.com/pod-product-compliance
Lightning Source LLC
Chambersburg PA
CBHW050824290526
45792CB00001B/248